Tricia

I loved all the poems, sayings &
Scriptures in this book.

I hope that you will enjoy
it as well. I am so
excited for you & Nathan & this
great Blessing Ethan that you
have been given! May God continue
to bless & Keep you.

Love Sheila

Published by Barbour Books, an imprint of Barbour Publishing, Inc., P.O. Box 719, Uhrichsville, Ohio 44683, www.barbourbooks.com

Member of the
Evangelical Christian
Publishers Association

Printed in China.
5 4 3 2 1

REJOICING WITH YOU IN THE BIRTH OF YOUR CHILD

KELLY KOHL

AND

LARISSA NYGREN

DayMaker
GREETING BOOKS

CONTENTS

Tricia & Nathan

As you rejoice in the birth of your child,
so do I!
Congratulations on the little bundle of joy
that God has entrusted to your care. . . .

My love & support
Sheila

When you were born,
you cried
And the world rejoiced.

NATIVE AMERICAN PROVERB

5

A NEW ADDITION
TO YOUR FAMILY

WHAT A BLESSING TO SEE YOUR FAMILY
GROW IN SUCH A BEAUTIFUL WAY!

ord, bless this new addition to our family.

NAME _____

DATE OF BIRTH _____

TIME _____

BABY'S WEIGHT _____

LENGTH _____

NOTES

_____

_____

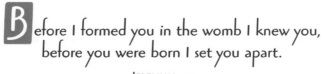

efore I formed you in the womb I knew you,
before you were born I set you apart.

JEREMIAH 1:5

Now we see but a poor reflection
as in a mirror; then we shall see face to face.
Now I know in part; then I shall know fully,
even as I am fully known.

1 CORINTHIANS 13:12

Perhaps the greatest social service
that can be rendered by anybody
to the country and to mankind
is to bring up a family.

GEORGE BERNARD SHAW

Holy as heaven a mother's tender love,
the love of many prayers and many tears
which changes not with dim, declining years.

CAROLINE NORTON

God could not be everywhere
and therefore He made mothers.

JEWISH PROVERB

Pride is one of the seven deadly sins;
but it cannot be the pride of a mother in her children,
for that is a compound of two cardinal virtues—
faith and hope.

CHARLES DICKENS

Training a child to follow Christ
is easy for parents. . .
all they have to do is lead the way.

AUTHOR UNKNOWN

Nothing I've ever done has given me
more joys and rewards
than being a father to my children.

BILL COSBY

Enjoy one another and take the time
to enjoy family life together.
Quality time is no substitute for quantity time.
Quantity time is quality time.

BILLY GRAHAM

LULLABY

Sleep, baby, sleep!
Thy father guards the sheep,
Thy mother shakes the dreamland tree,
And from it fall sweet dreams for thee;
Sleep, baby, sleep! Sleep, baby, sleep!

Sleep, baby, sleep!
The large stars are the sheep,
The little ones the lambs, I guess,
The gentle moon the shepherdess,
Sleep, baby, sleep! Sleep, baby, sleep!

Sleep, baby, sleep!
Our Savior loves His sheep,
He is the Lamb of God on high,
Who for our sakes came down to die,
Sleep, baby, sleep! Sleep, baby, sleep!

NORTH GERMAN LULLABY

Lord,
thank You for this blessed addition to our family.
Keep my baby safe from harm.
Let us never forget that she is a gift from You,
that she is Your beautiful creation.
Help us to put her into Your hands each and every day
so she may receive Your perfect love.
What a comfort, dear Father,
that we can depend on You
and Your Word for guidance
in caring for this new little life.
Amen.

THE JOY A BABY BRINGS

My first vivid memory is. . .
when first I looked into her face
and she looked into mine.
That I do remember,
and that exchanging of looks
I have carried with me all of my life.
We recognized each other.
I was her child and she was my mother.

PEARL S. BUCK

The great high of winning Wimbledon
lasts for about a week.
You go down in the record book,
but you don't have anything tangible to hold onto.
But having a baby—there isn't any comparison.

CHRIS EVERT LLOYD

*I love little children,
and it is not a slight thing when they,
who are fresh from God, love us.*

CHARLES DICKENS

Sometimes looking deep into the eyes of a child,
you are conscious of meeting a glance full of wisdom.
The child has known nothing yet but love and beauty.
All this piled-up world knowledge
you have acquired is unguessed at by her.
And yet you meet this wonderful look
that tells you in a moment more than
all the years of experience have seemed to teach.

HILDEGARDE HAWTHORNE

13

Father asked us what was God's noblest work. . . .
I said babies.

LOUISA MAY ALCOTT

When the baby laughed for the first time,
the laugh broke into a thousand pieces
and they all went skipping about,
and that was the beginning of fairies.

J. M. BARRIE, *Peter Pan*

We find delight in the beauty
and happiness of children
that makes the heart too big for the body.

RALPH WALDO EMERSON

14

We were filled with laughter,
and we sang for joy. . . .
Yes, the LORD has done amazing things for us!
What joy!

PSALM 126:2–3 NLT

A baby is an inestimable blessing. . . .

MARK TWAIN

What is overpowering is simply
the fact that a baby is life.
It is also a mess,
but such an appealing one that we
look past the mess to the jewel underneath.

BILL COSBY

15

A NEW LITTLE LIFE

A child's life is like a piece of paper
on which every person leaves a mark.

CHINESE PROVERB

He has achieved success who has loved much,
laughed often,
and been an inspiration to little children.

AUTHOR UNKNOWN

The potential possibilities of any child
are the most intriguing and
stimulating in all creation.

RAY L. WILBUR

People were bringing little children to him [Jesus]
in order that he might touch them;
and the disciples spoke sternly to them.
But when Jesus saw this,
he was indignant and said to them,
"Let the little children come to me;
do not stop them;
for it is to such as these that
the kingdom of God belongs.
Truly I tell you,
whoever does not receive the kingdom of God
as a little child will never enter it."
And he took them up in his arms,
laid his hands on them, and blessed them.

MARK 10:13–16 NRSV

ife is Love.

GOETHE

ife is not a holiday,
but an education.
And the one eternal lesson for us all is
how better we can love.

HENRY DRUMMOND

May the Lord make your love
increase and overflow for each other
and for everyone else,
just as ours does for you.

1 THESSALONIANS 3:12

LITTLE HEARTS. . .

Making the decision to have a child is momentous.
It is to decide forever to have your heart
go walking around outside your body.

ELIZABETH STONE

Soft is the heart of a child.

AUTHOR UNKNOWN

The mother's heart is the child's schoolroom.

HENRY WARD BEECHER

LITTLE HANDS. . .

The sweetest flowers in all the world—
A baby's hands.

ALGERNON CHARLES SWINBURNE

LITTLE FEET. . .

A baby's feet, like sea-shells pink
Might tempt, should heaven see meet,
An angel's lips to kiss, we think,
A baby's feet.

ALGERNON CHARLES SWINBURNE

A baby is born with a need to be loved and never outgrows it.

FRANK A. CLARK

To love and be loved is to feel the sun from both sides.

DAVID VISCOTT

Before you were conceived, I wanted you.
Before you were born, I loved you.
Before you were here an hour,
I would have died for you.
This is the miracle of life.

MAUREEN HAWKINS

21

THE BABY

Where did you come from, baby dear?
Out of the everywhere into the here.

Where did you get your eyes so blue?
Out of the sky as I came through.

What makes the light in them sparkle and spin?
Some of the starry spikes left in.

Where did you get that little tear?
I found it waiting when I got here.

What makes your forehead so smooth and high?
A soft hand stroked it as I went by.

What makes your cheek like a warm, white rose?
Something better than anyone knows.

Whence that three-cornered smile of bliss?
Three angels gave me at once a kiss.

Where did you get that pearly ear?
God spoke, and it came out to hear.

Where did you get those arms and hands?
Love made itself into bonds and bands.

Feet, whence did you come, you darling things?
From the same box as the cherub's wings.

How did they all just come to be you?
God thought about me, and so I grew.

But how did you come to us, you dear?
God thought of you, and so I am here.

GEORGE MacDONALD

LULLABY

Gracious Savior, gentle Shepherd,
Our little ones are dear to Thee;
Gathered with Thine arms and carried
In Thy bosom may they be
Sweetly, gently, safely tended,
From all want and danger free.
Tender Shepherd, never leave them
From Thy fold to go astray;
By Thy look of love directed,
May they walk the narrow way;
Thus direct them, and protect them,
Lest they fall an easy prey.

Let Thy holy Word instruct them:
Fill their minds with heav'nly light;
Let Thy love and grace constrain them,
To approve whate'er is right,
Take Thine easy yoke and wear it,
And to prove Thy burden light.
Cleanse their hearts from sinful folly
In the stream Thy love supplied;
Mingled streams of blood and water
Flowing from Thy wounded side;
And to heav'nly pastures lead them,
Where Thine own still waters glide.

JANE E. LEESON

Father,
thank You for the little life
You have entrusted to our care.
Not only have You created life in this child,
You have created new life in us as parents.
We feel twice as blessed
and are honored to rear Your sheep.
We will do our best in teaching our baby
of Your never-ending love
and will raise our family in thanksgiving of Your Son.
You will forever be a prominent presence
in our house, Lord,
as we will always take care
to appreciate Your many blessings.
May our baby always see You in our lives,
to know You more and better each day.
Amen.

HOPE FOR A BRIGHT FUTURE

The more people have studied
different methods of bringing up children
the more they have come to the conclusion
that what good mothers and fathers
instinctively feel like doing
for their babies is the best after all.

BENJAMIN SPOCK

Love and respect are
the most important aspects of parenting.

JODIE FOSTER

You should study not only that you
become a mother when your child is born,
but also that you become a child.

DOGEN

FOR A CHILD

Your friends shall be the Tall Wind,
The River and the Tree;
The Sun that laughs and marches,
The Swallows and the Sea.

Your prayers shall be the murmur
Of grasses in the rain;
The song of wildwood thrushes
That makes God glad again. . .

And you shall run and wander,
And you shall dream and sing
Of brave things and bright things
Beyond the swallow's wings.

And you shall envy no man,
Nor hurt your heart with sighs,
For I will keep you simple
That God may make you wise.

FANNIE STEARNS DAVIS

When you thought I wasn't looking,
I saw you hang my first painting on the refrigerator,
and I wanted to paint another one.
When you thought I wasn't looking,
I saw you feed a stray cat,
and I thought it was good to be kind to animals.
When you thought I wasn't looking,
I saw you make my favorite cake for me,
and I know that little things are special things.
When you thought I wasn't looking,
I heard you pray,
and I believed there is a God I could always talk to.
When you thought I wasn't looking,
I felt you kiss me good nights,
and I felt loved. . . .

When you thought I wasn't looking,
I saw tears come from your eyes,
and I learned that sometimes things hurt,
but it's all right to cry.
When you thought I wasn't looking,
I saw you give to someone needy
and I learned the joy of giving.
When you thought I wasn't looking,
I saw you always did your best
and it made me want to be all that I could be.
When you thought I wasn't looking,
I heard you say "thank you"
and I wanted to say thanks
for all the things I saw
when you thought I wasn't looking.

AUTHOR UNKNOWN

*I*nvest in the future;
have a child and teach her well.

AUTHOR UNKNOWN

*T*rain a child in the way he should go,
and when he is old he will not turn from it.

PROVERBS 22:6

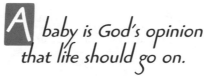

A baby is God's opinion
that life should go on.

CARL SANDBURG

The most important things
we can give our kids are our time,
our lives, and our values—
and values are caught more than they are taught.

TIM HANSEL

Acceptance and appreciation tell the child
that he or she is of tremendous worth.
And I can only express my acceptance
and appreciation through being affectionate—
and available.

JOSH MCDOWELL

Children are the living messages we send
to a time we will not see.

JOHN W. WHITEHEAD

Whatever you do,
put romance and enthusiasm
into the life of our children.

MARGARET RAMSEY MACDONALD

Children are one-third of our population
and all of our future.

SELECT PANEL FOR THE
PROMOTION OF CHILD HEALTH, 1981

Most important of all,
continue to show deep love for each other,
for love covers a multitude of sins.

1 PETER 4:8 NLT

your children will see what
you're all about by what you live
rather than what you say.
WAYNE DYER

We must teach our children to dream
with their eyes open.
HARRY EDWARDS

If children are to keep alive
their inborn sense of wonder,
they need the companionship of
at least one adult who can share it,
rediscovering with them the joy, excitement,
and mystery of the world we live in.
RACHEL CARSON

There are two lasting bequests
we can give our children:
One is roots.
The other is wings.

HODDING CARTER, JR.

The best inheritance you can leave your kids
is to be a good example.

BARRY SPILCHUK

We can't form our children on our own concepts;
we must take them and love them
as God gives them to us.

JOHANN WOLFGANG VON GOETHE

36

Children are
our most valuable natural resource.

HERBERT CLARK HOOVER

Each child is an adventure into a better life—
an opportunity to change
the old pattern and make it new.

HUBERT H. HUMPHREY

Children are apt to live up to
what you believe of them.

LADY BIRD JOHNSON

I hear babies cry.
I watch them grow.
They'll learn much more than I'll ever know.
And I think to myself,
What a wonderful world.

GEORGE D. WEISS AND GEORGE DOUGLAS

We began by imagining that
we are giving to them;
we end by realizing that
they have enriched us.

POPE JOHN PAUL II

LULLABY

Our children, Lord, in faith and prayer,
We now devote to Thee;
Let them Thy covenant mercies share,
And Thy salvation see.
Such helpless babes Thou didst embrace,
While dwelling here below;
To us and ours, O God of grace,
The same compassion show.
In early days their hearts secure,
From worldly snares, we pray;
O let them to the end endure
In every righteous way.

THOMAS HAWEIS

39

Lord,
now that You have blessed us with this child,
the future is of a far greater concern to me.
Please help me to raise my child
according to Your Word,
for if he follows You throughout his life,
he will always be heading toward
Your beautiful eternity.
I know the world can be a scary place, Lord,
and that his walk will not be an easy one,
but I also know that You will watch over him
and keep him in the palm of Your loving hand.
Father, help us all in our thoughts and actions,
so that we may, through You,
create a more loving, peaceful world.
Let my child reflect Your gracious love to others,
as I can only pray I will reflect Your love to him.
Amen.